THE RISE AND FA

THE
ISLAMIC
GOLDEN AGE
AND THE
CALIPHATES

JASON PORTERFIELD

ROSEN
PUBLISHING

NEW YORK

Published in 2017 by The Rosen Publishing Group, Inc.
29 East 21st Street, New York, NY 10010

Library of Congress Cataloging-in-Publication Data

Names: Porterfield, Jason, author.
Title: The Islamic golden age and the caliphates / Jason Porterfield.
Description: New York, NY : The Rosen Publishing Group, Inc., [2017] |
  Series: The rise and fall of empires | Includes bibliographical references
  and index.
Identifiers: LCCN 2015048641| ISBN 9781499463408 (library bound) |
ISBN
  9781499463385 (pbk.) | ISBN 9781499463392 (6-pack)
Subjects: LCSH: Islamic Empire'—History. | Caliphate—History.
Classification: LCC DS37.7 .P67 2017 | DDC 956/.013—dc23
LC record available at http://lccn.loc.gov/2015048641

Manufactured in China

CONTENTS

INTRODUCTION

The Islamic Empire arose spectacularly in the seventh century and quickly spread to cover a huge geographical area and exert a lasting influence on the course of history. Islamic dominance lasted from about 632 until about 1258 and extended across three continents—Europe, Asia, and Africa. The rulers, called caliphs, reigned over what was the world's largest empire at its height.

The catalyst for this unification and expansion was the introduction of the new religion of Islam by the prophet Muhammad. Muhammad's successors— the word "caliph" is derived from an Arab phrase for successor—conquered the lands surrounding the Arabian Peninsula and spread the new faith. Even as Islam served as a unifying banner that united people from a multitude of different backgrounds, divisions began to splinter the religion. Throughout the empire's existence, most rulers would be required to defend the empire with force. Some of these conflicts were fought with outsiders at the borders, but others were the result of internal turmoil. The rift between the Sunni and Shiite sects, in particular, resulted in periodic upheavals and was never resolved.

As the Islamic rule became more solidly established, a new Islamic civilization arose with its own rich culture and practices. The Islamic Empire absorbed influences from the

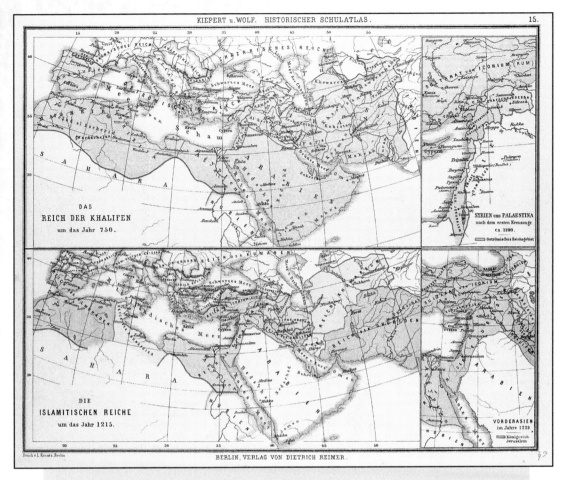

The Islamic faith, established in the 7th century, quickly spread beyond the Arabian Peninsula. Islamic culture, traditions, arts, and knowledge survived even as the empire's territory dwindled.

areas it conquered and saw new advances emerge from the new heterogeneous society. Arabic was introduced across the empire as the official language for administrative purposes. As intellectual life flourished, Arabic came to replace Greek as the universal language used by academics in science and philosophy.

The golden age of Islamic rule occurred during the early days of the Abbasid caliphate, which ruled from 750 until 1258. Following the collapse of the Umayyad caliphate in 750, the Abbasid caliphs established the new capital city of Baghdad in 762, and it quickly became a prosperous cultural center. Baghdad was renowned for its opulence as well as for arts and learning. The trade routes that brought wealth to the city also fostered an exchange of knowledge and allowed scholars from across the empire and beyond to travel to the court at Baghdad.

Abbasid power waned as the edges of the empire began to crumble into independent kingdoms. Overall, however, Islamic culture continued to thrive. Many Muslim rulers continued to support the arts and learning. But outside forces began to encroach on the Islamic realms. During the Crusades, which began in 1095, Christians from Europe led military campaigns against Muslims in the Middle East. During the thirteenth century, the Mongols invaded from Asia, sacking Baghdad in 1258. Today, the legacy of the caliphs lives on in the cultures and traditions established during their rule and in the creative and philosophical works generated during this vital historic era.

CHAPTER 1

THE ROOTS OF THE CALIPHATES

The age of Islam began in 622, the year of the prophet Muhammad's *Hijra*, or emigration, to Medina. Muhammad, founder and first leader of the faith, formed a community of his followers in his adopted city. The *Hijra* is such a significant event to Muslims that when Caliph Umar ibn al-Khattab introduced an Islamic calendar seventeen years later, the year 622 marked the beginning date.

Muhammad's leadership marked a new organization of society as well as the emergence of the Muslim faith. Before this point, Arabic society consisted of traditional tribes and clans. People were divided by economic and social class differences. Under Islam, they were united for the first time. Notably, Muhammad also allowed Christians and Jewish people to keep their faiths as fellow "People of the Book" and preached against inequality based on race and social class. Still, Islamic tolerance had its limits. Christian and Jewish subjects were in some cases subject to a tax—*jizya*—and people of other faiths were sometimes forced to convert later on.

ESTABLISHMENT OF ISLAM

Muhammad was born in 570 CE, an orphan raised by his uncle in the Arabian city of Mecca. He grew up to become a merchant, marry, and start a family, but his life was changed when he was visited by the archangel Gabriel in 610 CE. Muhammad had the revelation that he was the last prophet sent by God (Allah) to restore the true faith, which he preached as the teachings of the religion he called Islam.

Muhammad met resistance when he tried to spread Allah's message in Mecca. He sent a group of his followers to Abyssinia in present-day Ethiopia and Eritrea, where they found refuge from persecution. In 622, Muhammad traveled secretly to Medina in the flight known as the *Hijra*. His new faith grew quickly as the people of Medina embraced Islam.

War broke out between Muhammad's followers and the people of Mecca, who remained hostile to the Prophet and the Islamic

Muhammad's first revelation occurred when he was on retreat in a cave on Mount Hira. The angel Gabriel visited him in a dream and revealed a verse of the Quran.

faith. Muhammad's armies eventually conquered Mecca in 630. They continued conquering enemy tribes and converting many to Islam, taking control of the Arabian Peninsula, including the present-day countries Saudi Arabia, Yemen, Oman, and part of Jordan.

In 632, Muhammad traveled to Mecca, marking the first such *hajj*, or pilgrimage. He died in Medina later in the year, having succeeded in uniting the tribes of Arabia into a single nation.

STRUGGLE FOR CONTROL

When Muhammad died, he left behind a powerful political and religious state made up of the tribes of Arabia. Yet it remained to be seen whether the new religion and nation could survive without the Prophet and founder who served as the symbol of Islam to many of his followers. There was no clear successor in line to take over the leadership of the tribes and the Islamic faith.

After Muhammad's death, the Muslim community elected Abu Bakr al-Asamm, the father of Muhammad's wife and the Prophet's close friend, to serve as the first caliph of the Muslim-controlled territory. His official title was *khalifah rasul Allah*, or "successor of the messenger of god." The word *caliph* is derived from this term. A caliph is the political and religious successor to Muhammad and serves as the leader of the entire Muslim community. The caliph's right to rule the empire and serve as commander-in-chief was undisputed. The degree of the caliphs' religious authority, however, varied throughout the eras of various Islamic dynasties. Some Muslims preferred that religious scholars, not the caliph, oversee the traditions of Islam.

Even as Abu Bakr set out to serve as Muhammad's successor and continue his mission, bitter disagreements endured over who should rightfully claim the title of caliph. One group of followers thought that Muhammad's cousin Ali ibn Abi Talib should be the caliph, since he was Muhammad's closest living relative.

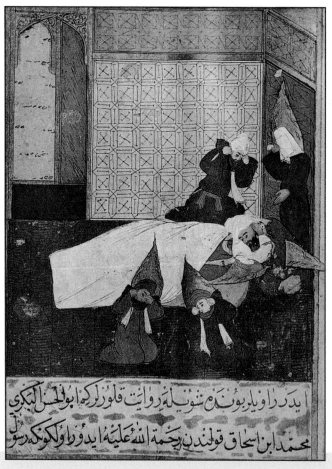

The prophet Muhammad is attended at his deathbed by Abu Bakr, his father-in-law and successor, the first Rashidun caliph.

THE SUNNI-SHIA SPLIT

The issue of succession following Muhammad's death ultimately caused a rift that divided Islam into two opposing branches. The Sunnis—"Ahl al-Sunna", the people of the tradition—made up the majority. They chose Abu Bakr as Muhammad's successor. The minority Shia— "Shiat Ali" or the party of Ali—believed that Muhammad's descendants, beginning with his kinsman Ali were the rightful leaders of Islam.

The split became irrevocable in 680, when Ali's son Husayn was killed during a battle with the Sunni caliph's forces. Marginalized by the Sunnis, who held political power, the Shia, or Shiites, followed leaders called imams. They rejected the legitimacy of the caliphs who succeeded Ali. The two branches also came to hold fundamentally different interpretations of Islamic theology and practices.

Today, the division endures, although the political disputes between the groups now overshadow their religious differences. The Shia are a minority group that make up less than 15 percent of the 1.6 billion worldwide followers of Islam. Nonetheless, conflicts between Sunnis and Shiites continue to cause strife in the Middle East and affect Islamic relations with the rest of the world.

THE RASHIDUN CALIPHS

Abu Bakr was the first of the four Rashidun, or "Rightly Guided," caliphs who ruled from Medina. Each of these caliphs were either elected or hand-picked by the previous caliph. The Rashidun led during turbulent times, as revolts arose among some of Muhammad's original followers, even while Muslim domination continued to spread across the region.

Abu Bakr ruled for two years after being elected Muhammad's successor. He solidified Muslim possession of Arabia and his armies attacked as far north as present-day Syria. Abu Bakr died in 634 of pneumonia.

His successor, Umar ibn al-Khattab, became the first leader to take the title of "caliph." Umar was also the father-in-law of Muhammad. A great conqueror, he captured more territory for the caliphate and occupied Jerusalem in 638. He went on to defeat the Persian Empire—which had long dominated the area comprising present-day Iran and, at its peak, stretched from as far as India to Egypt to Turkey and Armenia—seizing Damascus and Egypt. Umar was also known for his abilities as a lawmaker and an administrator who strengthened the organization of the growing state. He was killed by a Persian captive in 644.

The next caliph, Uthman ibn Affan, was nearly seventy years old when he was selected by a council. A member of Mecca's aristocratic and powerful Umayyad family, he had been Muhammad's son-in-law. He succeeded in expanding the territory under Muslim rule into present-day Iran and parts of Afghanistan, and he also invaded Armenia and northern Africa. Uthman is best remembered for compiling the Quran—the book regarded as the word of God by Muslims—into an authoritative version that is still used today.

Although he was initially popular among his people, discontent grew throughout his rule. As he aged, Uthman was no longer able to govern effectively. In addition, it was widely known that he practiced nepotism in granting important government positions to his kin in the Umayyad family. In 656, Uthman was assassinated by rebels led by the son of Abu Bakr, the first Rashidun caliph.

Uthman was succeeded by Ali ibn Abi Talib. He was Muhammad's cousin and had been passed over to succeed him when Abu Bakr became the first caliph. He resisted the idea of becoming caliph, but at meeting of warlords in Medina, they agreed he was the best equipped to lead the empire. Ali reluctantly took the post.

Ali's rule was brief and divisive. The Islamic territory—now an empire—was still in turmoil after Uthman's brutal assassination. Ali took no action to avenge Uthman's death despite the urging of many prominent Muslims. The empire devolved into civil war, and Ali was assassinated in 661.

Muslims consider the Quran a holy revelation received directly by Muhammad from Allah. Here, the 8th-century Quran of Uthman has been reproduced in 162 gold plates.

CHAPTER 2

ORDER FROM CHAOS

The Umayyad dynasty that claimed the caliphate after Ali's death ushered in a period of relative internal calm and even more expansion, during which Islam became the dominant religion of the Middle East. The Rashidun caliphs had ruled for fewer than thirty turbulent years after Muhammad's death. These decades were marked by the rapid growth of the caliphate through conquest, but also by civil war, upheaval, and assassinations. The Umayyad dynasty lasted for nearly ninety years, during which time it established a national government in a region that had previously been controlled on local levels by tribes and clans. The Umayyads also developed an administrative structure capable of managing the vast empire. Artistic traditions of the region began to emerge, influenced by the Byzantine and Sasanian Empires. Unlike the Rashidun caliphs, who lived simply, the Umayyad caliphs styled themselves as kings and surrounded themselves with wealth and opulence.

RISE OF THE UMAYYADS

Members of Caliph Uthman ibn Affan's family, the Umayyads, took control of the caliphate after Ali's death. A wealthy and powerful family of merchants, the Umayyads initially opposed Muhammad and his new religion of Islam. They converted when Muhammad's forces captured Mecca.

After Uthman's assassination, his nephew, Muawiyah ibn Abi Sufyan, demanded that his killers be brought to justice. Enraged by Ali's inaction, Muawiyah became one of his most bitter opponents during the civil war. Muawiyah was then governor of Syria and a skilled politician. His forces fought Ali to a stalemate, and Muawiyah defied Ali by declaring himself caliph. Briefly, two opposing caliphs ruled within the Islamic Empire before Ali's assassination. Ali's son Hasan abdicated the caliphate to Muawiyah in 661.

Although Muawiyah fought against the prophet Muhammad's forces in battle during the early years of Islam, he later became the caliph who succeeded in unifying the Islamic Empire. Here, he is received by an Arab queen, Mavia.

Despite the violent beginning to his rule, Muawiyah reigned during a period of relative peace and stability. He succeeded in reunifying the empire and moved the capital to Damascus, in Syria. Muawiyah continued to expand the borders of the Islamic Empire, as well. He sent armies across northern Africa, into northern India and central Asia. Caliphate ships even attacked Constantinople, capital of the neighboring Byzantine Empire, which lasted from 330 to 1453. The caliphates would periodically clash with Byzantines over the entire course of Islamic rule.

Muawiyah made the position of caliph hereditary, so that it would pass down through families. He named his son Yazid as his successor. When Muawiyah died in 680, however, he was succeeded during the next five years by three caliphs who all died shortly after taking control. During this period, the rulers became embroiled in another civil war with the followers of Ali, and ultimately, the caliphate passed to another branch of the Umayyad family.

THE UMAYYAD PEAK

The Umayyad dynasty reached its greatest period of strength during the rule of Abd al-Malik, who became caliph in 785. Abd al-Malik is considered by many to have been the most influential early Muslim leader to rule after Muhammad. He initiated many practices that set the Islamic Empire apart from the other dominant empires ruling during the same time.

The expansion of the Islamic Empire continued under Abd al-Malik, who unified the caliphate once again by putting down a rebellion among the Arab tribes of northern Syria and Iraq. He resumed the campaigns in northern Africa, fighting the native Berber tribes and conquering Carthage, the seat of the Byzantine Empire's territory in Africa. Abd al-Malik made careful political appointments, putting in place governors who could bring peace to particular areas.

During his long rule, Abd al-Malik overhauled some administrative aspects of the empire to make it run more efficiently. In the past, rulers had maintained the bureaucratic structures already in place in newly conquered territories. Abd al-Malik reorganized government departments and set up a system of collecting taxes and managing revenue. He established a postal service throughout the empire. Non-Muslim government officials were replaced with Muslims.

Two of his reforms were particularly important, both of them strengthening the Islamic character of the empire. Abd al-Malik made Arabic the official language of government across the caliphate. All official records would be kept in Arabic rather than Greek, Persian, or other languages prevalent in the sprawling empire. As a result, Arabic became more commonly spoken in many areas. Abd al-Malik also created a common currency for the empire. It was based on Greek and Persian money, but the coins were inscribed with texts from the Quran, rather than the rulers' images.

Abd al-Malik died in 705 and was succeeded by his son al-Walid. The new caliph continued the empire's expansion. Under his reign, the territory under Islamic rule spread east all the way to parts of central Asia and northern India. Al-Walid converted the Berber tribes to Islam and took control of parts of coastal northern Africa. The Berbers were the first large non-Arab group to come

One of the holiest sites in Islam, the Ummayad Mosque, was constructed by thousands of workers from across the empire. The octagonal Dome of the Treasury overlooks the courtyard.

under caliphate control—al-Walid made the caliphate an empire based on faith, not ethnicity. In 711, the Islamic Empire launched a conquest of Spain from Africa as the ruling Visigoths faltered. Al-Walid gave regional governors and local officials the freedom to govern as they saw fit.

Al-Walid is best remembered for the ambitious architectural projects inaugurated during his rule. He had many significant mosques built, including those in Medina and Jerusalem. In 706, he commissioned the great mosque at Damascus, which took a decade to build. It is now known as the Umayyad Mosque. Many distinctive features of Islamic architecture, such as domes, minarets, and arches, were developed during this period.

A patron of the arts, al-Walid promoted the first flourishing of Islamic court culture. He supported artists, writers, and musicians during his reign.

THE DOME OF THE ROCK

Caliph Abd al-Malik ordered the construction of the Dome of the Rock shrine in Jerusalem. Completed in 691, the site is sacred to both Muslims and Jews. The vast Dome was erected over a stone slab where Muslims believe that Muhammad began his ascension to heaven. Jews believe that the Biblical patriarch Abraham prepared to sacrifice his son Isaac on the stone.

The Dome of the Rock is the oldest existing Muslim monument, and it was the first Islamic structure that incorporated a dome. The building supporting the dome is

continued on next page

continued from previous page

octagonal, the interior and exterior decorated with mosaics and religious inscriptions that make up some of the earliest examples of Arabic writing. Because Islam traditionally forbids the representation of human and animal forms, the ornamentation does not include any images of people.

The Dome of the Rock is built over the Foundation Stone which, according to Jewish and Islamic tradition, overlies a chamber known as the Well of Souls.

FALL OF THE UMAYYADS

After Al-Walid died in 715, the Umayyad caliphate began unraveling. Al-Walid's brother Sulayman succeeded him as caliph. He sidelined or even executed many of the governors and generals who had served his brother well, sparking a distrust of the caliphate by the more distant reaches of the empire.

Sulayman continued the effort to expand Islamic territory, and he sent armies into Europe to attack the Byzantine Empire. He gained control of parts of eastern Europe and began the Siege of Constantinople in 717. Ultimately, the Islamic Empire gave up on any attempt to conquer the Byzantine Empire.

Sulayman died in 717 and was succeeded by his cousin Umar ibn Abd al-Aziz, the governor of Medina. Umar II was a pious ruler and a scholar who attempted to implement reform measures and unite Muslims across all ethnicities and branches of Islam. He implemented new taxation practices that treated Arab and non-Arab Muslims equally and ended the Umayyad practice of ritually cursing Ali, who was revered by Shiites. He continued charity programs begun by earlier caliphs and supported education. He also sent ambassadors to China and Tibet to invite rulers there to convert to Islam.

Umar's reforms and welfare programs made him a popular caliph who ruled during a period of stability, but they displeased some members of the Umayyad family. He died in 720, by some accounts, poisoned on his family's orders.

Umar II was replaced by his cousin, Yazid bin Abd al-Malik, known as Yazid II. He was a weak ruler, and his reign was marked by numerous civil wars breaking out throughout the caliphate, as many regional rulers rejected him. He died of tuberculosis in 724 and was replaced by his brother Hisham ibn Abd al-Malik.

Hisham ruled for more than 20 years and continued the reforms that began under Umar II and the support of the arts of al-Walid. He built schools and oversaw the translation of literature and science texts into Arabic. Despite his capable rule, he was unable to solve the problems threatening to tear the empire apart. He faced internal unrest and military setbacks on the Iberian Peninsula against the Khazars in eastern Europe and a major revolt by the Berbers in northern Africa. When he died in 743, the golden age of Umayyad prosperity ended.

He was succeeded by three caliphs who further destabilized the empire during their brief reigns. The last Umayyad ruler, Marwan II, became caliph in late 744. In 747, he faced an uprising led by the Abbasid family who also included Persian, Iraqi, and Shiite Muslim forces. The Umayyad army was defeated in 750 at the Battle of the Great Zab River in Iraq. Marwan II fled to Egypt and was killed there shortly after. Nearly all other members of the Umayyad family were hunted down and massacred except for Abd al-Rahman, who fled to Spain and established a separate kingdom, the emirate of Córdoba. The first caliph of the new Abbasid dynasty began his reign in 750.

Hisham ibn Abd al-Malik built many palace complexes in Resafa in present-day Syria, an ancient town that today exists only as an archaeological site.

CHAPTER 3

THE GOLDEN AGE

Despite the dynasty's bloody beginnings, the Abbasids ushered in the most influential age of the Islamic Empire. The era is remembered for the prosperity and opulence of the great city of Baghdad and the achievements of its scientists, mathematicians, and philosophers. While the period from 500–1000 is sometimes called Europe's Dark Ages, scholars in the Islamic Empire preserved knowledge passed down from ancient Greece and made their own advancements.

Like the Umayyads, the Abbasid caliphs surrounded themselves with opulence far removed from their subjects. The grand capital city of Baghdad was designed to set the caliph apart from the people of the city.

The days of the Islamic Empire's territorial expansion had passed, but trade and the exchange of knowledge flowed within its vast borders and beyond during its golden age. Eventually, however, inward turmoil and the increasing independence of outlying regions of the empire led to the Abbasids' decline.

ABBASID DOMINANCE

The Abbasids laid hereditary claim to the caliphate based on their descent from Abbas, who had been the prophet Muhammad's uncle. The family remained on the sidelines of public affairs for many generations. During the later years of the Umayyad rule, the revolutionary movement recruited Abbas' great grandson, Muhammad ibn Ali, to their cause. Various rebel factions united in opposition to the Umayyads. In particular, many resented the caliphate's policies that favored Arab Muslims over non-Arabs. The Abbasids succeeded in attracting a wide allegiance.

Muhammad ibn Ali's son, Abu al-Abbas, led the Abbasid forces in Kufa, in present-day southern Iraq. He declared himself caliph there in 749. The next year, following the overthrow of the Umayyads, he claimed formal control of the entire caliphate and took the name al-Saffah, or "bloodshedder." Much of his reign, as well as that

A bronze head of Abu Jaafar Abd Allah al-Mansur stands in Baghdad's Mansur district, which was named for the caliph who founded the city in 762.

of his successor's, was spent in putting down insurrections. For non-Arab Muslims and the minority Shiites, who had been the Abbasids' allies during the revolution, the new regime failed to meet their expectations of transformation. The Shia developed into an opposition sect.

Present-day Iraq became the center of Islamic politics and culture. Al-Saffah established the capital in Kufa and then Anbar, and he set about rebuilding the caliphate. He allowed Jews, Christians, and Persians to join the government and reformed the army to allow non-Muslim and non-Arab soldiers. Al-Saffah also restored emphasis on education and set up a paper-making industry in Samarkand, which contributed to a rise in literacy. Al-Saffah died in 754, and his brother al-Mansur became caliph.

BAGHDAD FLOURISHES

Al-Mansur proved himself a wise and diligent ruler, and a period of stability followed al-Saffah's reign. Al-Mansur succeeded in bringing the contentious region of Syria under his control through a combination of suppression and payments. Many non-Arabs converted to Islam during this period, and Arabs lost their key positions of influence within the government. The Abbasid tolerance for Persians and other ethnic and cultural groups within the caliphate led to a growth in Persian scholarship and literature. Al-Mansur also established a palace library, where scholars would translate works into Arabic, and he invited scholars from India to share knowledge of astronomy and mathematics.

Al-Mansur's changes to the government, especially his promotion of non-Arabs and his tendency to look toward the East (toward Persia and present-day Turkey) rather than the West (toward Africa and southern Europe), established a solid foundation that would be maintained by his immediate successors. In the long-term, however, these policies would contribute to the destabilization of the empire.

Al-Mansur is best remembered for establishing a new imperial capital in Baghdad, founded in 762. It was a walled city accessed by four huge iron gates. The caliph's palace and a mosque occupied the center, and the city provided a base for the caliphate's extensive administrative bureaucracy. Baghdad's location on the Tigris River helped it develop into a major cultural and commercial hub. The city quickly grew beyond its walls to include sprawling suburbs.

Al-Mansur died in 775 while on pilgrimage to Mecca. His son, al-Mahdi succeeded him after his death and continued his policies, retaining the loyalty of his father's advisors and governors. He was a pious ruler who oversaw the restoration of many mosques, but he also supported poets and musicians in his court. Baghdad grew rapidly at that time, welcoming newcomers from Syria, Arabia, Persia, and as far away as Spain and Afghanistan. Muslims, Christians, Jews, Zoroastrians, and Hindus lived together peacefully in the capital.

Al-Mahdi died in 785. His son, the celebrated Harun al-Rashid, became caliph in 786 after the short, troubled reign of his brother, al-Hadi.

THE HOUSE OF WISDOM

Al-Rashid presided as caliph at the height of the Abbasid rule, during which time Baghdad became the richest and one of the most cultured cities of the world. The empire was relatively peaceful during his reign, and the expansion of trade and industry brought prosperity to the realm. Al-Rashid largely delegated his authority to his vizier and other key officials, although he wielded ultimate power over their decisions. A family called the Barmakids, in particular, greatly contributed to many of the accomplishments credited to al-Rashid as well as the previous caliphs al-Mansur and al-Mahdi. The Barmakids served the Abbasids loyally and competently for generations and became fabulously wealthy.

Al-Rashid's reign was not altogether free of internal volatility, and some events presaged future instability. Al-Rashid left Baghdad in 796 and largely governed from Al-Raqqah in Syria while working to control rebellions in that region. In 800, he agreed to allow Ibrahim ibn al-Aghlab considerable authority to govern a region in northern Africa in return for a large annual tribute payment, which led to the foundation of a separate Aghlabid dynasty. This arrangement benefited the caliphate's treasury at the cost of meaningful sovereignty. Eventually, the pattern would be repeated elsewhere in the further reaches of the empire, leading to a reduced area of influence. In 803, al-Rashid ordered the Barmakid family imprisoned and their wealth seized.

Souverains parmi le peuple.
Haroun-al-Raschid se mêle au peuple incognito.

The Abbasid caliph Harun al-Rashid is best remembered for his persona in *Arabian Nights*, in which he frequently disguised himself and mingled with his subjects during his adventures.

Still, al-Rashid presided over many great achievements. He established a library called Bayt al-Hikma (House of Wisdom), expanding the translation program beyond medicine, mathematics, and astronomy to include other subjects. It developed into a scholarly institution that sought to interpret, preserve, and add to works of scientific and philosophical understanding. Books and manuscripts were highly prized, and scholars enjoyed special status. Tributes paid by lesser rulers to the caliphate funded al-Rashid's art and architecture programs.

When al-Rashid died in 809, the caliphate was split between his two sons. Al-Amin became caliph, and al-Mamun governed the eastern province of Khorasan, but civil war broke out. Al-Mamun's army beseiged Baghdad for a year, and al-Amin was killed when the city fell. Al-Mamun became caliph in 813.

THE BOOK OF ONE THOUSAND AND ONE NIGHTS

Harun al-Rashid is more widely known today for his mostly fictionalized adventures in *A Thousand and One Nights*—also called *Arabian Nights*—than for his historical reign. Disguised as a commoner and joined by his real-life friend Jafar the Barmakid, he joins pages shared by the exploits of Ali Baba, Aladdin, Sinbad the Sailor, and many others.

A Thousand and One Nights was compiled by the Baghdad scholar al-Jahshiyari

The tales in the *Arabian Nights* include romances, comedies, tragedies, adventures, and fantasy stories, many set in Baghdad during Harun al-Rashid's reign.

continued on next page

continued from previous page

in the tenth century. The story begins when the queen Scheherazade is condemned to die by her husband, the sultan Schahriar. The night before her execution, she tells a story to her sister so that the sultan will overhear. She stops before she finishes the tale, and the curious sultan allows her to live another day so that she can tell the rest the next night. Scheherazade repeats this pattern for a thousand and one nights, until the sultan relents and removes the death sentence.

Al-Jahshiyari based his work on an old Persian text called *Hazar Afsana* (*A Thousand Tales*), made up of stories originating in ancient India. He added tales from the oral folk traditions of Persia, Egypt, and Arabia, and incorporated historical figures into the narrative, setting many escapades and romances in al-Rashid's court. Other writers continued adding tales to *A Thousand and One Nights* until it reached its present form in the late 15th century.

Al-Mamun, himself an intellectual, continued the work of the House of Wisdom. The institution attracted scholars from many different places and across disciplines. Texts were translated from Greek and other languages, and intellectuals traveled to distant lands to collect manuscripts. Scholars at the House of Wisdom kept the official calendars, worked as engineers and architects, served as consultants to the caliph, and practiced medicine. The first public hospital had been founded in Baghdad under al-Rashid, and more were subsequently established in other major cities.

The scholars at the House of Wisdom also performed groundbreaking research in many fields. They absorbed ancient learning from works such as translations of Archimedes, Ptolemy, and Euclid, and they went on to make their own advances. Al-Mamun commissioned projects to map the world, study the Egyptian pyramids, and determine the circumference of the earth. Scholars introduced numerals from India, which are now known as Arabic numerals. The great scholar al-Khwarizmi developed the mathematical branch of algebra. The scientist and philosopher al-Kindi wrote hundreds of treatises on subjects ranging from optics to music to an attempt to reconcile religion and philosophy. The three Banu Musa brothers produced important works on geometry and mechanics, including the *Book of Ingenious Devices*.

The scholars at the House of Wisdom preserved ancient texts and made their own contributions to science—knowledge that eventually spread to Europe.

Al-Mamun directed construction of the first observatory in the Islamic world, and astronomers at the House of Wisdom improved the designs of instruments used in astronomical observation such as the astrolabe and sundial. Today, many stars in the heavens still bear Arabic names.

WARFARE AND DECLINE

Al-Mamun reigned during a period of continued stability of the Islamic Empire, but some of his decisions caused dissent and discontent. During the early years of his caliphate, he attempted to rule from the western city of Merv rather than from Baghdad. Rebellions forced him to return to Baghdad. Al-Mamun increasingly began to depend on military forces recruited from the west, especially Turks, rather than Arabs, as had been traditional. He also tried to reconcile the Shiites with the Sunni caliphate, but his attempts failed to win over the Shiites and succeeded only in alienating members of his Abbasid family. Al-Mamun broke with tradition when he asserted his authority in theological affairs, demanding that all Muslims follow a certain doctrine. The caliph's interference and persecution of dissenters caused controversy and division. Meanwhile, many governors of outlying provinces came to be granted more authority in return for tribute paid to Baghdad, making the caliph's rule merely nominal.

Upon al-Mamun's death in 833, his brother al-Mutasim became caliph. Al-Mamun's successors faced near-continual warfare. Al-Mutasim expanded on al-Mamun's practice of maintaining a military force primarily loyal to the caliph. Many of these soldiers were bought as Turkish slaves, and al-Mutasim's reliance on them exacerbated the division between the ruler and his subjects of the Islamic Empire. The people of Baghdad resented the foreigners, and rioting broke out in 836.

Al-Mutasim built a new capital city of Samarra north of Baghdad, in part to avoid civil unrest. Samarra served as the Abassid's capital for the next sixty years. The caliphs became increasingly isolated from the Islamic people. The Turkish forces around the caliph became increasingly powerful.

Samarra served as the capital of the Islamic Empire for less than a century before the caliphs returned to Baghdad. The well-preserved site, with ruins of the Caliphal Palace, was designated a World Heritage Site in 2007.

Al-Mutasim was succeeded in 842 by his son al-Wathiq, who continued most of his father's policies, including support of intellectual pursuits and the arts, especially music. Al-Wathiq was succeeded in 847 by his brother al-Mutawakkil, who reversed many policies of his predecessors. He ousted their ministers, reversed al-Mamun's pronouncement on religious doctrine, persecuted the Shiites, ended tolerance of Jews, Zoroastrians, and Christians, and had no interest in art or learning. Al-Mutawakkil did, however, have a passion for grand architecture. During his lifetime, his builders completed at least twenty new palaces and the Great Mosque of Samarra, known for its spiral minaret.

Al-Mutawakkil was assassinated in 861 by Turkish soldiers conspiring with his son al-Muntasir, who succeeded him as caliph. Al-Muntasir himself was found dead of unknown causes six months later. The era of the great Abbasid caliphate, with its vast empire, had ended.

CHAPTER 4

THE SPLINTERING CALIPHATE

The Abbasid caliphate began declining rapidly after al-Mutawakkil's death. Regional governors in more distant parts of the empire had been granted more autonomy to govern on their own since the reign of al-Mahdi. A few territories began to split off and form their own independent states without recognizing the authority of the Abbasid caliphate.

The early breakaway rulers did not call themselves caliphs. The Umayyad dynasty established in Spain in 756, for example, called itself an emirate—a state led by a dynastic ruler that could either exist independently or comprise part of a larger political entity.

Later on, however, the population of the Islamic world started to grow alienated from the Abbasid caliphs. Many of the outlying parts of the empire were too far away for effective central administration. Closer to the empire's heart, the caliphs lost the wide support of the Muslim people, who no longer saw their beliefs and priorities embodied in inaccessible rulers dominated by their private armies. The Abbasids were increasingly weakened and irrelevant, and independent states grew emboldened. The Fatimid dynasty established a caliphate to challenge the Abbasids in 909, and the Spanish Umayyad dynasty proclaimed itself a caliphate in 929.

RULERS OF SPAIN

The first part of the Islamic Empire to become independent was in present-day Spain. A single member of the

Umayyad dynasty, Abd al-Rahman, escaped the Abbasid massacre in 750. Destitute, he wandered through Egypt and northern Africa before crossing over to the Iberian Peninsula. Once there, he raised an army of Arabs living in Spain who were still loyal to the Umayyads. In 756, after years of internal conflict, al-Rahman defeated the Abbasid governor and founded the emirate of Córdoba.

Abd al-Rahman, the "Falcon of Andalus," succeeded in subduing resistance to his rule and founding a long-reigning dynasty in Spain.

The new state covered most of the Iberian Peninsula, including nearly all of Spain. Its capital, Córdoba, was in the region of al-Andalus—present-day Andalusia in Spain. The emirate of Córdoba endured longer than the other independent states, surviving as an emirate until 929 as a seat of the Umayyad dynasty. At that point, al-Rahman's descendant, Abd al-Rahman III, extended the emirate's lands into northern Africa and named himself caliph of Córdoba. The Muslims of mixed Spanish, Berber, and Arabic origin came to be called Moors.

Spain experienced a golden age under the rule of the Umayyads. Members of different religions managed to coexist peacefully, although Arabs were accorded certain rights not granted to Jews and Christians. Universities were founded in many major cities. The height of culture and learning occurred during the eleventh and twelfth centuries. Scholars made advances in the study of geography, science, history, and philosophy. Poetry, literature, the arts, and architecture thrived.

The capital of Córdoba was one of the greatest cities in the world during its zenith. Opulent palaces, mosques, and public baths were constructed. The Great Mosque was one magnificent example; it was later converted into a Roman Catholic cathedral. The city was also at the center of economics and trade, and its artisans crafted fine leather, jewelry, and textiles.

The caliphate endured until 1031, when civil wars broke out and the state broke into several smaller kingdoms. Subsequently, the reigning Muslims were defeated

The Great Mosque of Córdoba was constructed in the 780s during the reign of Abd al-Rahman, and it has served as a Roman Catholic cathedral since 1236.

by Christian forces. The first major Islamic city to be overtaken was Toledo, which fell in 1085. In 1236, Christian forces seized Córdoba. The last vestige of Moorish power in Spain was extinguished when the city of Granada fell to the Christians in 1492.

THE IDRISID DYNASTY

In northern Africa, the first Shiite dynasty took power in the late eighth century in parts of present-day Morocco and Algeria held by Berber tribes. Its founder was Idris I, who claimed to be a descendent of the prophet Muhammad and Ali. He fled after the Abbasid rulers subdued an unsuccessful Shiite uprising near Mecca in 786. Idris I escaped to Morocco, where a Berber tribe called the Awraba took him in and made him their imam (religious leader). The countryside was mostly Muslim, but it was still dominated by Berber language and customs.

Idris I organized the Awraba and subjugated non-Muslims living in the region. In 789, he founded the Idrisid dynasty, establishing the city of Medinat Fas as his capital. Idris I cut ties to the Abbasids and welcomed Arabs to the region to help govern his kingdom. In 791, however, he was assassinated on orders of the Abbasids, leaving a young son.

His son, Idris II, took power in 803. He gave the capital the new name of Fez and oversaw its development into a major trading post. The city became a religious and cultural center with two mosques and a university. Upon the death of Idris II in 828, however, power was divided among eight of his sons, fracturing the kingdom and leading to a decline of Idrisid power.

Berber tribes began a series of uprisings against the Idrisids in 868. The attacks and loss of territory weakened the kingdom. With the establishment of the Fatimid caliphate in northern Africa in the early tenth century, the Idrisid rulers were caught in the middle of conflicts between the Fatimids and the Umayyad caliphate of Córdoba. The Idrisids lost Fez in the 920s. The last Idrisid ruler was defeated by the Umayyads in 974 and executed in 985. Although the Idrisids had largely become assimilated into Berber society, the dynasty left behind an Arab influence on cities and towns of northern Africa.

THE SILK ROAD

The Silk Road was a network of trade routes that linked the East to the West from about the second century BCE to the fifteenth century. It spanned from China to the Mediterranean Sea, with seaways looping around the Arabian Peninsula. Traders traveling along parts of its 4,000 miles (6,000 km) of routes exchanged luxury goods such as silk and ceramics as well as spices, precious metals, and animals. Beginning in the 700s, the western sections of the Silk Road were dominated by the Islamic Empire.

The Silk Road served as a vital cultural exchange, facilitating the sharing of ideas and knowledge. Technologies spread from one region to another—for example, papermaking techniques were probably brought to Samarkand, in present-day Uzbekistan, from China. Pilgrims and missionaries traveled along the road for religious purposes, and migrants and traders took their faiths with them to new lands. In this way, Islam, as well as Christianity, Buddhism, and Hinduism, became more widely practiced across Eurasia.

THE FATIMID CALIPHATE

During the late eighth century, a radical branch of Shia, called Ismailism after the imam Ismail, arose. After decades of insignificance, the Ismailis began to acquire political power in Yemen. A minority in the Abbasid caliphate established themselves in northern Africa beginning in the late ninth century. The Ismaili leaders claimed to be descended from Muhammad's daughter, Fatimah bint Muhammad.

In 909, the Fatimids established a separate caliphate based in northern Africa that rejected the authority of the Abbasid caliph on religious grounds. The founder, Ubayd Allah al-Mahdi Billah, ruled as caliph of a new state made up of part of present-day Tunisia. He joined forces with the Berbers to conquer present-day Algeria. The caliphate expanded under several of al-Mahdi Billah's successors to include Sicily, Morocco, and the lands of the Idrisid caliphate. Over time, the Fatimids would take control of northern Jordan, Yemen, Lebanon, Syria, Palestine, and, briefly, Baghdad. At its height in the mid-eleventh century, the dynasty's territory included most of the eastern Mediterranean coast from the Red Sea to the Atlantic Ocean.

In 969, the Fatimids conquered Egypt and moved their capital from the city of Al-Mansuria in present-day Tunisia to Cairo. The Fatimids developed extensive trade networks in the Indian Ocean and throughout the Mediterranean, and the dynasty had diplomatic ties with China's ruling Song dynasty. Cairo grew into a prosperous city that was the cultural center of Islam at the time. Fatimid craftsmen were known for ceramics, metalworking, and glassware. The caliphs supported learning and the arts. They founded universities—including Al-Azhar University, Egypt's oldest—as well as libraries and astronomical observatories. The renowned astronomer Ibn Yunus worked under the Fatimid dynasty. The caliphate was tolerant of Sunnis and non-Muslims and would appoint them to government posts based on merit.

The Fatimid caliphate began to decline after its capture of Baghdad from 1057 to 1059. Like the Abbasids, the caliphs

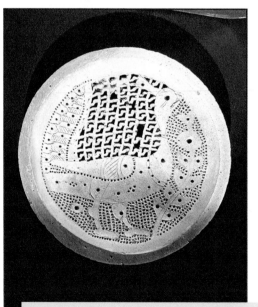

had come to depend on their armies to maintain Fatimid rule. Differences arose between various factions of the army, especially Berber and Turk elements. The army collapsed, and a long famine struck Egypt around 1060, leading to internal strife. After a lengthy period of civil warfare, the caliphate dissolved in 1171.

A pottery water filter from Fatimid Egypt is decorated with a peacock, a symbol of good life. The device kept a bottle of water cool and free of insects.

CHAPTER 5

THE LAST OF THE ABBASIDS

The Abbasid dynasty remained in control of the caliphate even as parts of the empire broke away. Some of the family's stronger rulers, including al-Mansur, Harun al-Rashid, and al-Mamun, had let some parts of the empire govern themselves in order to avoid yet more civil wars. Even so, the breaking away of northern Africa and rising dissatisfaction among various groups in Persia and Syria gradually weakened the dynasty.

Government revenue declined because of reduced taxes and tribute flowing in from the shrinking empire. The Abbasid caliphs became near puppets of their Turkish army leaders. After al-Mutawakkil's assassination in 861, he was succeeded by four caliphs within a decade, who were all killed by the Turkish military—on one

43

occasion by soldiers rioting after failing to be paid. The Abbasid dynasty endured until 1258, but the caliphate's role as the dominant power of the vast Islamic empire had ended.

TROUBLE AT HOME

At their peak, the Abbasids ruled over an empire that stretched across southern Europe, northern Africa, the Middle East, and deep into Asia. While distant parts of the caliphate were splintering away, the Abbasids had to deal with internal problems in Arabia and Persia. In 869, the black slaves of southern Iraq called the Zanj rebelled, seizing territory and even threatening Baghdad. The rebellion was quelled in 883, and Baghdad was restored as the Abbasids's capital city, ushering in a brief period of stability.

By the mid-tenth century, following several coups and struggles for control, the Abbasids's authority was reduced to the area surrounding Baghdad. As powerful dynasties emerged around them, the Abbasids nearly lost control of Iraq. The most immediate threat was the Buyid dynasty that came to power in Persia. In 945, the Buyid army marched into Baghdad and easily occupied the city. The Abbasid caliph was forced to grant the position of *amir al-umara* (emir of emirs) to the Buyid leader. For the next century, the Buyids ruled from Baghdad while controlling the Abbasid caliph and providing him with a small allowance. Although the Buyids were Shiites, they retained the nominal power of the Sunni Abbasid caliphate for political reasons.

LOSS OF STATUS

Even as the Abbasids remained in Baghdad as figure-head leaders, the Abbasid caliphate broke up into separate states. Africa was lost to the Fatimid dynasty. In 977, the Ghaznavid dynasty of Turkish origins took control of the eastern parts of the caliphate, establishing their region's dynasty in Ghazna in present-day Afghanistan. Their territory included parts of Iran and extended into northern India. The real power in Persia remained in the hands of the Buyids. Abbasids kept their court culture and retained symbolic significance, but they had lost the attention of political and religious leaders.

Nonetheless, Islamic culture continued to thrive. The Buyids were tolerant of religious diversity, and Persian poetry and literature flourished. Islamic states maintained support of learning and the arts, and the exchange of knowledge continued within the former boundaries of the empires. The various emirates introduced innovations in models of government. Some of Islam's greatest scholars lived and worked during this period. The tenth-century physician al-Majusi wrote the landmark treatise *The Complete Book of the Medical Art*, which discussed psychological as well as physical disorders. The great Persian philosopher and physician Ibn Sina (known in the West as Avicenna), who died in 1037, also made contributions in many other fields of science. In the caliphate of Córdoba, Ibn Rushd (known in the West as Averroes) wrote on philosophy and theology as well as other topics in science, medicine, and mathematics during the twelfth century.

A 17th-century edition of the *Canon of Medicine* by Ibn Sina (also called Avicenna) depicts the preparation of a treatment for a smallpox patient.

RISE OF THE SELJUQS

The Buyid dynasty lasted until 1055, when the family was weakened by internal fights and defeated by the Seljuq dynasty. The Seljuqs were a Sunni Muslim family of Turks who had adopted Persian culture. In 1037, Turks had swept

down from central Asia to found the Seljuq empire. Once installed in Baghdad, they put an end to the fighting that had kept the city in constant turmoil.

As Sunnis, the Seljuqs recognized the religious authority of the Abbasid caliphate. They allowed the Abbasids to retain their title of caliph. A Seljuq, however, would be placed the new position of sultan, or military defender of the faith, and would wield the real power in Baghdad.

The Seljuqs ushered in a revitalization of the Islamic Empire that is sometimes called the Sunni revival. The new rulers launched military offenses against the neighboring Byzantines and forced them to draw back. Eventually, the Seljuqs held most of present-day Iran, Iraq, Palestine, and Syria. The period of Seljuq rule was marked by a highly religious character, and many theological schools and mosques were constructed under the dynasty.

THE CRUSADES

The Seljuqs posed a real threat to the Byzantine Empire, and Emperor Alexius Comnenus asked Pope Urban II for military assistance from the Catholic Church. The pope responded in 1095 by launching a large-scale attack against the Seljuqs that would come to be known as the First Crusade. Urban preached the importance of seizing lands that were controlled by Muslims but that the church considered holy. He gathered forces from across Europe for the attack. To the Seljuqs and other Muslims, it was an unexpected invasion that they were too disorganized to

Richard the Lionheart (left), king of England, and the Muslim military leader Saladin are depicted in mounted combat during the Third Crusade (1189–1192).

face. This crusade began a series of attacks and counter-attacks that spanned about 100 years and resulted in three separate crusades, as Christian and Muslim armies fought over territories, particularly the holy city of Jerusalem. The great Muslim general Saladin was able to unify opposition to the Crusaders, and in 1187 he took control of the holy city of Jerusalem. He and the crusader King Richard II of England worked out a treaty that kept the city in Muslim hands, but promised safety to Christian pilgrims.

REVIVAL AND FALL

In the twelfth century, the Abbasid dynasty succeeded in briefly regaining political power and relevance. As the Seljuq dynasty faltered, Caliph al-Mustarshid led a rebellion against the Seljuqs in 1135, but he was defeated and killed. His successor, Caliph al-Muqtafi, also raised an army and managed to seize parts of Iraq from the Seljuqs, repelling a long siege of Baghdad in 1156. Caliph al-Nasir took control of all of Iraq from 1180 until his death in 1225.

Al-Nasir attempted to restore the former glory of the Abbasid caliphate. He achieved relative peace by making shrewd alliances and maintaining order with a military organization called the *futuwwa*. Baghdad became a center of learning once again.

The period of stability was fleeting. Invading Mongol tribes led by Genghis Khan were already sweeping across Asia and toward the Middle East during al-Nasir's lifetime.

In 1258 Genghis Khan's grandson Hulegu Khan destroyed Baghdad and killed the last Abbasid caliph.

The golden age of Islam ended with the Mongol invasion, but the Abbasid dynasty was not altogether extinguished. The Mamluks, who were the descendants of the Turkish soldiers of al-Mamun's army, reestablished an Abbasid caliphate in Cairo in 1261 with surviving members of the family. This caliphate survived until 1517, but its power was ceremonial only.

The Mongols laid siege to Baghdad in 1258, after which the army slaughtered the citizens, plundered its valuables, destroyed the libraries, and set the city ablaze.

LEGACY OF THE CALIPHS

The caliphates were a dominant force in the Middle East for about 300 years and remained influential up through the end of the Abbasids. Their legacy endures today in many ways.

- **Arts:** The caliphates spread distinct styles of painting, architecture, textiles, and literature throughout their territory.
- **Scholarship:** The House of Wisdom allowed scholars to make new advance in mathematics, medicine, geography, astronomy, and philosophy.
- **Transmission of knowledge:** Scholars preserved Greek and Roman works that might otherwise have been lost during Europe's Middle Ages.
- **Government:** The bureaucracy established by the caliphates served as a model for later governments.

In addition, key religious and political events of the age remain relevant to the present day. The schism between Shiite and Sunni Muslims continues to generate friction around the world. To this day, people invoke the term "Crusades" in discussing tensions between Christians and Muslims. However, while the long history of the caliphates includes many sequences of factional clashes, it also provides models for tolerance among populations of diverse religious and cultural backgrounds.

622 The Prophet Muhammad flees from Mecca to Medina, an event known as the *Hijra*.

632 The Prophet Muhammad dies. The caliphate is founded with Abu Bakr's election as Muhammad's successor.

632–61 The Rashidun (Rightly Guided) caliphs rule.

661 Ali is assassinated.

661–750 The Umayyad caliphs rule.

685–701 Abd al-Malik rules during a period of expansion and administrative reform.

691 The Dome of the Rock shrine is completed.

711 Muslim forces occupy Spain.

717 The Islamic empire gives up on any attempt to conquer the Byzantine Empire after the unsuccessful Siege of Constantinople.

750 The Abbasids defeat the Umayyad rulers. The Abbasid dynasty is established, with al-Saffah the Abbasid caliph.

756 Abd al-Raḥman establishes the emirate of Córdoba in Spain.

762 Al-Mansur founds Baghdad as the empire's new capital.

786–809 Harun al-Rashid rules as the fifth caliph of the Abbasid dynasty. The Bayt al-Hikma (House of Wisdom) is established.

789 Idris I founds the Idrisid dynasty in northern Africa.

803 Al-Rashid orders the Barmakid family imprisoned and their wealth seized.

813–33 Al-Mamun rules as caliph.

833–42 Al-Mutasim rules as caliph.

836 The capital is moved to the new city of Samarra.

847–61 Al-Mutawakkil rules as caliph and is assassinated by Turkish soldiers.

869–83 The Zanj slaves revolt in southern Iraq; the rebellion is quelled.

892 The Abbasid capital is restored to Baghdad.

909 The Fatimids establish a caliphate in northern Africa.

929 Abd al-Rahman III names himself caliph of Córdoba in Spain.

945 The Buyid army marches into Baghdad and occupies the city.

945–1055 The Buyid dynasty holds a position of sovereignty in Baghdad.

969 The Fatimids conquer Egypt and moved their capital to Cairo.

974 The Idrisid kingdom falls to the Umayyads of Córdoba.

1031 The caliphate of Córdoba collapses.

1037 The Seljuq empire is established.

1055 The Seljuqs occupy Baghdad and establish it as the capital of the Seljuq empire.

1095 European Christians launch the First Crusade against the Seljuqs.

1156 Abbasid caliph Al-Muqtafi repels a long siege of Baghdad by the Seljuqs, reclaiming parts of Iraq.

1171 The Fatimid caliphate collapses.

1180–1225 Al-Nasir rules as caliph and reinstates Abbasid control over all of Iraq.

1187 Saladin recaptures Jerusalem from the Crusaders.

1219 The Mongols invade central Asia and eastern Persia.

1258 Mongols sack Baghdad and put an end to the Abbasid Dynasty.

1261–1517 A nominal Abassid caliphate is maintained in Cairo.

assassinate To kill someone, especially for political or religious motives.

astrolabe An early scientific instrument used to observe and determine the position of celestial bodies.

caliph An Islamic ruler considered the successor of Muhammad.

conquer To acquire or take control of through military force.

Crusade One of the military expeditions led by European Christians against Muslims in the Middle East between the eleventh and thirteenth centuries.

dynasty A succession of hereditary rulers of a country.

emirate A state ruled by an Islamic ruler called an emir, an often hereditary position.

ethnicity A group of people with common cultural characteristics, such as a religion or language.

faction A group of people within the main body of a larger group, such as a political party or government.

hajj The pilgrimage to Mecca required of all Muslims and one of the Five Pillars of Islam.

Hijra The emigration of the prophet Muhammad to Medina as he and his followers fled persecution in Mecca. The year of the persecution, 622, marks the beginning of the Muslim calendar.

imam An Islamic religious leader.

invade To enter forcibly, especially as a military campaign against an enemy.

jizya The tax non-Muslim citizens of an Islamic government are required to pay.

minaret A tower connected to a mosque with one or more balconies from which Muslims are called to prayer five times a day by a crier.

mosque A Muslim place of worship.

pilgrimage A long journey taken for religious purposes.

prophet A person who claims to speak the will of God.

rebellion An armed or violent uprising against an established government or other authority.

reign A sovereign's period of rule.

revenue A government's income, from sources such as taxation, that is used to pay for public expenses.

sect A religious group, especially an offshoot of an established religious denomination.

successor One who takes over a position or office from another.

sultan A Muslim ruler of a state, especially a Turkish sovereign.

theology The study and analysis of religious doctrines and the existnece of God.

treatise A written discourse on a particular subject, often thorough and systematic.

tribute A payment made from one leader or state to another, usually to one that is more powerful.

vizier A high ranking official or minister in the service of a caliph or Islamic leader.

Institute of Islamic Studies
McGill University
Morrice Hall, Room 319
3485 McTavish Street
Montreal, QC H3A 0E1
Canada
(514) 398-6077
Website: https://www.mcgill.ca/islamicstudies/
The main focus of the Institute of Islamic Studies is the disciplined
   study of Islamic civilization throughout the scope of its history and
   geographical spread.

International Museum of Muslim Cultures
201 E. Pascagoula Street
Jackson, Mississippi, 39201
(601) 960-0440
Website: http://www.muslimmuseum.org/
The International Museum of Muslim Cultures aims to educate the
   public about Islamic history and culture and the contributions of
   Muslims to world civilizations.

IslamiCity
P.O. Box 3030
Culver City, CA 90231
(310) 642-0006
Website: http://www.islamicity.com/
IslamiCity's mission is to share with the world an understanding of
   Islam and Muslims and to promote peace, justice, and harmony for
   all people.

Islamic Society of North America (ISNA)
P.O. Box 38
Plainfield, IN 46168
(317) 839-8157

Website: http://www.isna.net/
The ISNA aims to foster the development of the Muslim community,
  interfaith relations, civic engagement, and better understanding of
  Islam.

The Metropolitan Museum of Art—Islamic Art Department
1000 Fifth Avenue
New York, New York 10028
(212) 535-7710
Website: http://www.metmuseum.org/about-the-museum
  /museum-departments/curatorial-departments/islamic-art
New York's Metropolitan Museum of Art has a large collection of
  Islamic works of art on display, some of which can be viewed
  online.

National Council of Canadian Muslims (NCCM)
P.O. Box 13219
Ottawa, ON K2K 1X4
Canada
(866) 524-0004
Website: http://www.nccm.ca/
NCCM is dedicated to protecting the human rights and civil liberties
  of Canadian Muslims (and by extension of all Canadians), promot-
  ing their public interests and challenging Islamophobia and other
  forms of xenophobia.

WEBSITES

Because of the changing nature of Internet links, Rosen Publishing
has developed an online list of websites related to the subject of
this book. This site is updated regularly. Please use this link to access
this list:
http://www.rosenlinks.com/RFE/islam

FOR FURTHER READING

Al-Hassani, Salim T.S., ed. *1001 Inventions: The Enduring Legacy of Muslim Civilization*. Washington, D.C.: National Geographic, 2012.

Ansary, Mir Tamim. *Destiny Disrupted: A History of the World Through Islamic Eyes*. New York, NY: PublicAffairs, 2010.

Campo, Juan Eduardo. *Encyclopedia of Islam*. New York, NY: Facts On File, 2009.

Clark, Malcom. *Islam for Dummies*. Hoboken, NJ: Wiley, 2011.

El Cheikh, Nadia Maria. *Women, Islam, and Abbasid Identity*. Cambridge, MA: Harvard University Press, 2015.

Esposito, John. *What Everyone Needs to Know About Islam*. New York, NY: Oxford University Press, 2011.

Etheredge, Laura, ed. *Islamic History*. New York, NY: Britannica Educational Publishing, 2010.

Haddawy, Husain, trans. *The Arabian Nights: Alf laylah wa-laylah*. New York, NY: W.W. Norton, 2008.

Hazleton, Lesley. *After the Prophet: The Epic Story of the Shia-Sunni Split in Islam*. New York, NY: Anchor Books, 2010.

Hazleton, Lesley. *The First Muslim The Story of Muhammad*. New York, NY: Riverhead Books, 2013.

Kuiper, Kathleen, ed. *Islamic Art, Literature and Culture*. New York, NY: Britannica Educational Publishing, 2010.

Le Strange, Guy. *Baghdad: During the Abbasid Caliphate*. New York, NY: Cosim Classics, 2011.

Madden, Thomas F. *The New Concise History of the Crusades*. Lanham, MD: Rowman & Littlefield, 2013.

Mahfouz, Naguib. *Arabian Nights and Days*. New York: Doubleday, 1995.

Nasr, Seyyed Hossein. *The Study Quran: A New Translation and Commentary*. New York, NY: HarperCollins, 2015.

O'Kane, Bernard. *The Civilization of the Islamic World*. New York, NY: Rosen Publishing, 2013.

Ruthven, Malise. *Islam: A Very Short Introduction*. New York, NY: Oxford University Press, 2012.

Seddon, Mohammed, and Raana Bokhari. *The Illustrated Encyclopedia of Islam: A Comprehensive Guide to the History, Philosophy and Practice of Islam*. London, England: Lorenz Books, 2010.

Silverstein, Adam J. *Islamic History: A Very Short Introduction*. New York: Oxford University Press, 2010.

Stefon, Matt, ed. *Islamic Beliefs and Practices*. New York, NY: Britannica Educational Publishing, 2010.

BIBLIOGRAPHY

Ball, Warwick. *Out of Arabia: Phoenicians, Arabs and the Discovery of Europe*. Northampton, MA: Olive Branch Press, 2010.

BBC. "Muslim Spain (711–1492)." September 4, 2009 (http://www.bbc.co.uk/religion/religions/islam/history/spain_1.shtml).

BBC. "Sunnis and Shia: Islam's ancient schism." June 20, 2014 (http://www.bbc.com/news/world-middle-east-16047709).

Bennison, Amira K. *The Great Caliphs: The Golden Age of the 'Abbasid Empire*. New Haven, CT: Yale University Press, 2009.

Bobrick, Benson. *The Caliph's Splendor: Islam and the West in the Golden Age of Baghdad*. New York, NY: Simon & Schuster, 2012.

Cardini, Franco. *Europe and Islam*. Malden, MA: Blackwell Publishers, 1999.

Hill, Fred James, and Nicolas Awde. *A History of the Islamic World*. New York, NY: Hippocrene Books, Inc. 2003.

Kennedy, Hugh. *When Baghdad Ruled the Muslim World: The Rise and Fall of Islam's Greatest Dynasty*. Cambridge MA: Da Capo Press, 2004.

Lyons, Jonathan. *The House of Wisdom: How the Arabs Transformed Western Civilization*. New York: Bloomsbury Press, 2009.

Rahman, H.U. *A Chronology of Islamic History, 570–1000 CE*. Boston, MA: G.K. Hall & Co., 1989.

Robinson, Francis, ed. *The Cambridge Illustrated History of the Islamic World*. New York, NY: Cambridge University Press, 1996.

Shuster, Mike. "The Origins Of The Shiite-Sunni Split." *NPR*, June 16, 2014 (http://www.npr.org/sections/parallels/2007/02/12/7332087/the-origins-of-the-shiite-sunni-split).

Spuler, Bertold. *The Age of the Caliphs: History of the Muslim World*. Princeton, NJ: Markus Wiener Publishers, 1995.

Wood, Frances. *The Silk Road: Two Thousand Years in the Heart of Asia*. Berkeley, CA: University of California Press, 2002.

INDEX

INDEX

ABOUT THE AUTHOR

Jason Porterfield is an author and journalist living in Chicago. He has written more than twenty books for Rosen, including the titles *Islamic Customs and Culture and Scandinavian Mythology*. Jason graduated from Oberlin College with majors in English, history, and religion, and he remains fascinated by the dynasties that once ruled the Islamic world.

PHOTO CREDITS

Cover, p. 1 Nicola Messana Photos/Shutterstock.com; p. 5 Universal History Archive/Universal Images Group/Getty Images; p. 8 Topkapi Palace Museum, Istanbul, Turkey/Bildarchiv Steffens/Bridgeman Images; p. 10 ullstein bild/Getty Images; p. 13 AFP/Getty Images; pp. 15, 22 De Agostini Picture Library/Getty Images; p. 18 Tim Gerard Barker/Lonely Planet Images/Getty Images; p. 20 Kyrylo Glivin/Shutterstock.com; p. 24 Ahmad Al-Rubaye/AFP/Getty Images; p. 28 Private Collection/Bridgeman Images; p. 29 Culture Club/Hulton Archive/Getty Images; pp. 31, 48 Print Collector/Hulton Archive/Getty Images; p. 33 Heritage Images/Hulton Archive/Getty Images; p. 36 Private Collection/ © Look and Learn/Bridgeman Images; p. 38 JTB Photo/Universal Images Group/Getty Images; p. 42 Werner Forman/Universal Images Group/Getty Images; pp. 46-47 DEA/G. Dagli Orti/De Agostini/Getty Images; p. 50 DEA/J.E. Bulloz/De Agostini/Getty Images; interior pages background image © iStockphoto.com/somnuk
Designer: Brian Garvey; Editor: Shalini Saxena; Photo Researcher: Nicole Baker